IT'S A NEW SEASON

GET STARTED AFRESH TODAY

VICTORIA DAVID

Copyright © 2020 by Victoria David

All rights reserved

Victoria David has asserted her right to be identified as the author of this Work in accordance with the Copyright, Designs and Patents Act 1988

All rights reserved. No part of this publication may be reproduced, stored in a retrieval system or transmitted in any form or by any means, electronic, mechanical, photocopying, recording or otherwise, without the prior permission of the copyright holder or the Copyright Licensing Agency.

Unless otherwise stated Scripture quotations taken from the Authorized (King James) Version. Rights in the Authorized Version in the United Kingdom are vested in the Crown. Reproduced by permission of the Crown's patentee, Cambridge University Press.

Cover photo by Chi Liu on Unsplash

CONTENTS

Foreword	v
Acknowledgements	vii
Introduction	ix
1. Behold I Make ALL Things New	1
2. Time to Let Go of the Old	7
3. New Wine in the New Wine Skin	23
4. Ministry of Angels in the New Season	39
5. Made New By The Blood Of Jesus	63
6. Divine Recovery in the New Season	71
7. How to Stay Focused in Your New Season?	81
8. Prayer of Repentance	95
9. Daily Decrees and Declarations for Transformation in the New Season	99
About the Author	107

FOREWORD

It's A New Season, is an eye and spirit opener to what the Holy Spirit of the Lord is saying at this time to everyone all over the world. In 1 Chronicles 12:32a we are told, "And of the children of Issachar, which were men that had understanding of the times, to know what Israel ought to do". As people of God we need to have discernment about our times and season and what we should be doing. And the author did an exceptional work of enlightenment through this book about how our world is changing and how the Spirit of the Lord is saying expressly that it's a time of reset for all things and that God is a God of the new. This book will awake in anyone that reads it the consciousness that holding on to the past is a waste of resources, time and energy, but by depending on God,

FOREWORD

we can embrace the amazing new opportunities and blessings every new day brings our way.

This book is also to encourage everyone that we can't afford to be stuck on the same level. Even if you feel you are doing well at the moment, but as the author has said with God's help we must seize the new privileges of each new day that God intends to move us from one level of Glory to another. Maybe currently, you feel you are by yourself and you do not have physical help, there is good news. You have supernatural support in God and the angelic host. So everyone must be excited to embrace the changing NEW PARADIGMS of our time to profit according to heaven's agenda for this season.

Finally, I strongly believe that all of us should appreciate the revelation, insight, inspiration and labour of Victoria David in producing this book. It's God's heartbeat for us. And for anyone that has spiritual understanding, it's truly a New Season for all humanity.

Olugbenga David
Founder & Senior Pastor
Covenant and Glory Ministries International (CGMI)

ACKNOWLEDGEMENTS

I thank my heavenly FATHER, the Lord Jesus Christ and Holy Spirit for their direction and help in writing this book. Frankly, I would not have been able to put it together without them. For it is in them I live, I move and have my being.

INTRODUCTION

When we wake up from our sleep each morning, GOD presents us with a brand new day. The new day tells us that yesterday has gone and has become our past. The brand new day is filled with GOD's seen and unseen blessings and His endless opportunities to do things better. The new day comes with an opportunity to love better than we did yesterday, to work better than we did before and to forgive those that have hurt us.

Today, even, is the new day the LORD has given unto mankind loaded with HIS blessings, loaded with HIS goodness, loaded with HIS mercies, loaded with fresh ideas and fresh opportunities to start anew. Today can be a beginning for a new season for you. A season

INTRODUCTION

where GOD will give you beauty for ashes and turn your sorrow into great joy. Today did not arrive empty-handed but it came loaded with grace for us to enter into a new season in life. Let us look at Isaiah 43:18–19:

> "Remember ye not the former things, neither consider the things of old.
>
> Behold, I will do a new thing; now it shall spring forth; shall ye not know it? I will even make a way in the wilderness, and rivers in the desert."

You can see that the LORD was telling HIS people Israel to forget the former things, the things of the past, and not to consider the things of old but rather to focus on the NEW things HE is doing in their lives. In other words, HE did not want them to worry about past incidents and issues that might have weighed them down. But rather HE wanted them to concentrate on the things HE is doing for them now. He did not want them to concern themselves any longer with what was, but rather with what is. HE wanted them to focus on the things HE was doing for them at the time, looking at the now and not the past.

The LORD was encouraging HIS people Israel to put

INTRODUCTION

the past behind them and let it go. HE said to them that, HE will do a new thing for them and it shall spring forth NOW and not tomorrow. HE continued by reminding them that, HE is GOD Almighty and HE can do ALL things. HE can even make a way in the wilderness and rivers in the desert for them. Which is to say, HE can do what is seemingly impossible to man, for HE is The I AM THAT I AM, The Almighty GOD.

I believe that Isaiah 43:18-19 is not only applicable to the children of Israel, but is also applicable to us, the Body of Christ, today. We can see from these scriptures that the LORD wants His children to let go of the past, the old things, and the former things and embrace the new. Lamentations 3:23 tells us that the mercies of GOD are new every morning and great is HIS faithfulness.

The LORD is saying to you and me today that HE will do a NEW thing in us. We should let go of the former things that have weighed us down, the things that stopped us from enjoying the blessings and benefits HE bestows upon us daily. It is time to let go of the former things and allow the LORD to beautify our lives with HIS goodness.

ONE
BEHOLD I MAKE ALL THINGS NEW

In January 2019 on two different occasions, when spending time with HIM, the LORD told me twice that HE is going to do a new thing in my life. HE said to me, "Look unto ME, for all that you desire and your desires shall be granted. It shall be very well with you. I shall do a new thing in you, watch out for the new thing I will do for you. It shall spring forth. Behold, I make ALL things new. I will teach you from now on new ways of doing things in your marriage, ministry, career and life. It is a new beginning for you from now on. Forget about the old and embrace the new in ME."

Since then, I started to experience GOD's inner peace like never before. The Holy Spirit also reminded me that He had laid it in my heart to write this book the year before. He said to me, "Go ahead and write it, I will help you to write it because it needs to be written in this season." So, I quickly went to retrieve my notes from my notepad.

I find it amazing that since that moment, every time I turn on the television and watch the Christian channels there is a message about the new thing GOD is doing on earth or the new thing HE is going to do in HIS church and the world as a whole. I started seeing the word "New" everywhere I went, even on the walls of my home. I believe the LORD is about to pour out a fresh wave of HIS glory in our lives and also in HIS church. HE is also going to do a new thing on the earth that all eyes will behold.

Let us look at the meaning of the word new. The word can mean "not in existence before", "having recently come into existence", "unfamiliar", "being other than the former or old", "now for the first time". It could also mean "produced", "introduced", or "discovered recently" (online dictionary).

According to the above interpretations, when the LORD is saying HE is going to do a new thing, I believe HE is saying, HE is going to do something that is not in existence already. He is going to do some things in your life and mine, things that have never been seen or done. And these things shall spring forth suddenly. Part of Isaiah 43:19 says "now" it shall spring forth. Not tomorrow or the day after but "now". So, we need to position ourselves to receive the new things the LORD is about to do in our lives now. We are now in the season of a new thing. The new wine skins are upon us.

GOD is about to replace the old, the former, those things which has seen service, the marred and worn out with the new. 2 Corinthians 5:17 says, "Therefore if any man be in CHRIST, he is a new creature, old things are passed away, behold, all things have become new." The day we gave our lives to the Lord Jesus and made Him our Lord and our Saviour, we are made new in Him. The minute we give our lives to the Lord He wants us to put on the new man we have now become in Him. He wants us to do away with the "old man" and his old ways. To be able to do this we must renew our minds with the word of GOD daily. No wonder we are told in Ephesians 4:23, that we are to be renewed in the spirit of our mind.

Interestingly, in Romans 12:2, we are told that we should not conform or comply with the ways of this world but rather we should be transformed, metamorphosed or changed by the renewing of our mind, that we may prove what is the good, acceptable, and perfect will of GOD. We need a changed mind to be able to enjoy and experience the new things the LORD is doing in our lives. The LORD does not want us to be weighed down with our past problems, past failures, past relationships, past disappointments, past mistakes, past errors when we are in our new season. But rather, HE wants us to be present in our now, so that we can enjoy our new season of love, mercy, joy, forgiveness, peace and rest in HIM. For it is in Him we live, we move and have our being.

In Revelation 21:5, the LORD tells us that HE will make all things new:

> "And he who was seated on the throne said, 'Behold, I am making all things new.' Also he said, 'Write this down, for these words are true and faithful.'"

Notice the LORD is using the present tense in this verse of Scripture, "I am making all things new". GOD is doing a better thing than what was before.

Old things have passed away. Behold all things have become new.

The LORD is doing a new thing in the earth today. HE is pouring out a new wave of HIS glory in HIS church. With this new wave of glory will come miracles, signs, wonders and breakthroughs that we have not heard of before. In 1 Corinthians 2:9 we are told, "But as it is written, eye has not seen, nor ear heard, neither have entered into the heart of man, the things which GOD has prepared for them that love HIM." The LORD is telling us here that there is more HE has for HIS children, especially those that love HIM. All we need to do is to yield to the Holy Spirit of the living GOD and receive everything HE is downloading in our spirit in the new season we are in now.

TWO
TIME TO LET GO OF THE OLD

In this new season, the LORD wants us to open our hearts to HIM to receive from HIM what HE has for us. Someone might be asking: what does the LORD have for us in this new season? Could it be new strategies to fight the good fight of faith? Or could it be that the Lord has new strategies for our businesses, careers, marriages, for raising up our children, or whatever else it may be, to be turned around for good? Why don't you ask HIM today to show you new strategies of dealing with things in a better way this new season? For, HE is the Alpha and Omega and the author and the finisher of our faith.

We need to do away with our old ways of doing things in our own strength and logic and start to depend on

GOD and listen attentively to what HE is saying to us in this new season. We must start to yield to the Holy Spirit and follow His instructions and leading consistently, so that we can win the battles of life and become all that GOD has called us to. Proverbs 3:5-6 tells us that we should trust in the LORD with all our heart, and lean not on our own understanding. For when we acknowledge HIM in all our ways, HE will make our paths straight. When we trust in the LORD and recognise HIM in everything that we do, HE promise to guide our steps, make our paths straight and not crooked. For HE is a faithful GOD, who wants us as HIS children to rely upon HIM in all that we do.

GOD wants to rewire our minds to align our thoughts with the new things HE is doing and going to do in us as the body of Christ. If GOD is rewiring our minds, we need to consciously lay our ear on HIS chest to listen to what HE is saying to us in this new season. I strongly believe that as we start renewing our thoughts in HIS word daily, HE will heal us from our past wounds, mistakes, offences and abuses. He will heal our brokenness and create new pathways for us to walk in. GOD wants to deliver us from our past so that we can enjoy our new season and abundant blessings HE has prepared for us. But we need to be ready and cooperate with HIM and allow HIM to remould us to become all that HE has created us to be.

Romans 12:2 tells us that we should not conform to this world's ways of doing things but we are to renew our minds to be able to live a transformed life in Christ Jesus:

> "And be not conformed to this world: but be ye transformed by the renewing of your mind, that ye may prove what is that good, and acceptable, and perfect, will of GOD."

When you look at the word "renew" we can see that it is prefixed by the word "re". The prefix "re" is added in front of words to mean "again" or "to do again". The word "new" means "different from the one that existed earlier" (online dictionary).

So, what does the scripture tells us when it says we have to renew our minds? To change our old or former ways of doing things, we need to change our minds and start thinking differently from the way we use to think before, by the renewing of our minds. We are to be transformed by the renewing of our minds, so that we can express in ourselves that good, acceptable, and perfect will of GOD.

New Beginning of Authority

In the Old Testament, the LORD revealed to Joshua that Moses had died as a way to encourage him from not to look at the past but to start looking forward towards the future. HE also told Joshua, that an old era had gone and a new era of authority was just beginning. Now, the LORD said to Joshua, arise and cross this Jordan with all the children of Israel I have put in your leadership, unto the Promised Land. The LORD was encouraging Joshua like HE is encouraging you and me today that he was living in a new era. And like Joshua, today is a new day, a new season, a new beginning, and a time for new leadership. It is time to let go of yesterday, its former things, embrace today with courage and the changes it brings.

> "Now after the death of Moses the servant of the LORD it came to pass, that the LORD spake unto Joshua the son of Nun, Moses' minister, saying, Moses my servant is dead; now therefore arise, go over this Jordan, thou, and all this people, unto the land which I do give to them, even to the children of

Israel. Every place that the sole of your foot shall tread upon, that have I given unto you, as I said unto Moses. From the wilderness and this Lebanon even unto the great river, the river Euphrates, all the land of the Hittites, and unto the great sea toward the going down of the sun, shall be your coast. There shall not any man be able to stand before thee all the days of thy life: as I was with Moses, so I will be with thee: I will not fail thee, nor forsake thee. Be strong and of a good courage: for unto this people shalt thou divide for an inheritance the land, which I swear unto their fathers to give them. Only be thou strong and very courageous, that thou mayest observe to do according to all the law, which Moses my servant commanded thee: turn not from it to the right hand or to the left, that thou mayest prosper withersoever thou goest."

(JOSHUA 1:1-7)

We see in the above scriptures, the LORD informing Minister Joshua that it is a new beginning of authority, "for Moses my servant is dead." HE was making it plain to Joshua that Moses is dead and he should stop looking out for him because he is gone and will never return. The LORD was making a point to Joshua that, Moses' era had passed with yesterday and today starts another new era. HE was telling Joshua that he is now the new leader HE has appointed to replace Moses the great. It is time for Joshua to go over this Jordan to continue where Moses stopped. It is now your turn to lead the children of Israel to the Promised Land. Arise Joshua arise.

I believe the LORD is speaking to the Joshuas of this new era and new season to ARISE and go to that assignment HE has called you to. Could it be that GOD has an assignment HE has created for you and you are looking back at yesterday? It is time for all the Joshuas of this new era to summon up the courage to ARISE and go to the assignment that GOD has for you to accomplish. In verse 7, the LORD told Joshua to be strong and VERY courageous. In order to embrace the new, especially in leadership, means that we need to be strong and courageous. It is my prayer for you today that the LORD Almighty who has called you in HIS Vineyard will strengthen and give you the courage you need, to ARISE to HIS assignment for your life, in the mighty name of Jesus.

In the book of Samuel, the Prophet Samuel was still mourning Saul's rejection by GOD when the LORD

IT'S A NEW SEASON

told him to fill up his horn with oil and go to the house of Jesse and anoint the new king to replace Saul. Could it be that the Prophet Samuel was holding on to the past even when GOD had begun a new thing in Israel? This is like many of us holding on to past glories, things that GOD has already condemned, places HE had told us to move from, toxic friendships and relationships we should separate ourselves from, employments and assignments that HE had clearly told us to leave behind and move on to the next task HE has for us. Even when the LORD is saying to us GO, your assignment here is done, we still hang on to dead things of the past, that the LORD is separating us from. It might be that you are like Samuel, still looking at the past, GOD would have you to start looking to the future, for the new king is waiting for you to be anointed.

I believe the LORD is saying to someone right now that you have been in this mountain for too long, it is time to crossover to the Jordan to go and take hold of your possessions. It is time to arise and go to the Promised Land. It is time to listen to the LORD and move on to the New assignment HE has for you in this New Era.

When GOD says it's a new beginning of authority, HE

is saying to us, I AM giving you another chance to make it better today than you did yesterday. HE is saying to us, I have a new opportunity for you today that was not available to you yesterday. HE is saying I have opened a new door for the old one that was closed. HE is saying it is time for you to move on to the new level of grace, new level of glory, new level of favour and new level of riches, new level of prosperity and new level of wealth. All we have to do now is to say yes to the LORD, let YOUR will be done in my life today FATHER as it is in heaven.

The Renewed Mind

I believe that the renewed mind is the mind of Christ. The renewed mind is the transformed mind. The renewed mind is the repented mind that is ready to say goodbye to the old life and embrace the new life in Christ Jesus. The renewed mind is about seeing things the way the LORD sees things. It is about aligning our thoughts with GOD's thoughts. It's also about having a higher perspectives of life. Not self-defeating thoughts or patterns but embracing the mind of Christ. The renewed mind is a powerful mind that can change the trajectory of your destiny. The

Scriptures tell us in 1 Corinthians 2:16b that we have the mind of Christ.

The renewing of our mind is done supernaturally by the help of the Holy Spirit. In Romans 8:5-6 we are told that those who live according to the flesh set their minds on the things of the flesh, but those who live according to the Spirit set their minds on the things of the Spirit. For to be carnally minded is death, but to be spiritually minded is life and peace.

In this new season we are in, we need to live our lives according to the Spirit and things of the Spirit. If we continue to live by the flesh, after we have given our lives to Jesus, this will lead to spiritual death and sometimes, even, to physical death too. But living spiritually minded lives lead to life and peace in Christ Jesus.

We are told in Colossians 3:8-10 that, we should now also put off all these things behind us: anger, wrath, malice, blasphemy, filthy communication and lie not one to another, seeing that we have put off the old man with his deeds. It goes further to say that we should put on the new man, which is renewed in knowledge after the image of HIM that created us.

We are to do away with the old man with his sinful ways of doing things and clothe ourselves with the new man. So that we can increase in divine knowledge after the image of GOD our creator.

We need to renew our minds so that we do not miss what the LORD has for us in the new season. Because it is no longer going to be business as usual and we are no longer going to do things as we use to do them before. This is the time for us to let go of the old and embrace the new. As we do so, the LORD will give us divine strategies to overcome old ways of doing things. He will give us new strategies for a successful marriage, better parenting skills, divine leadership strategies, divine business strategies, divine revelations and winning ways and ideas to do things. But the key to all these blessings is by yielding to the Holy Spirit and walking in His ways and not by our own understanding.

As we renew our minds in this new season, we should remember to put on the mind of Christ. It is also the time to move from the past into the present with a renewed sense of strength, a renewed joy, a renewed love for the Lord Christ Jesus, a renewed courage, a renewed zeal and a renewed mind in the LORD.

When our minds are renewed, we obtain the mind of Christ and start thinking on things that builds our faith rather than on self-defeating thoughts and the lies of the devil. When our minds are renewed, we start thinking positively, as we are instructed by Apostle Paul in Philippians 4:8:

> "Finally, brethren, whatsoever things are true, whatsoever things are honest, whatsoever things are just, whatsoever things are pure, whatsoever things are lovely, whatsoever things are of good report; if there be any virtue, and if there be any praise, think on these things."

In this verse, the first thing Apostle Paul tells us to do is to meditate on the things that are true and not on things that are false. We should not meditate on the lies of the enemy but on what the word of GOD says about us. True things are the things that align with GOD'S promises and blessings for us His children.

Secondly, he tells us that we should meditate on those things that are honest. We should focus our mind on things that are moral, honourable and integral. According to the Cambridge dictionary, the word honest means, "(of a person) truthful or able to be trusted; not likely to steal, cheat, or lie". So as

Christians we are expected to focus our renewed mind on things that are sincere and not on insincere things.

Thirdly, after meditating on those things that are honest, the next thing the Apostle Paul encourages us to meditate on are things that are just. What are just things? Just things are those things that are in consonance with justice and righteousness. Romans 8:4 tells us that the righteousness of the law might be fulfilled in us who walk not after the flesh, but after the Spirit of the living GOD. The renewed mind is a mind that is just and righteous, that thinks not after the flesh but after the Spirit of GOD.

Fourthly, he tells us that we should meditate on the things that are pure and not on impure or adulterated things. Pure things are holy things; they are uncontaminated. 2 Corinthians 7:1 tells us that "having therefore these promises dearly beloved, we should cleanse ourselves from all filthiness of the flesh and spirit, perfecting holiness in the fear of GOD." To walk in purity as Christians we must do away with all filthiness and embrace holiness. Hebrews 12:14 tells us to "follow peace and holiness with all men and without these no man can see the LORD."

The fifth thing the Apostle Paul tells us to meditate on are lovely things. He admonishes us to meditate on whatsoever things that are lovely, these are the things that we should focus our minds on. Lovely things are pleasing and beautiful things. They are pleasant and not hideous. Lovely things are also godly things that are pleasing unto our GOD.

Good report is the sixth thing he lists that we should meditate on. It is important for us to meditate on good reports and not on negative reports that can cause us anxiety and even send us into depression. We should focus our minds on the praiseworthy things that will encourage us and remind us of the goodness of our GOD. Good reports gives us joy and motivates us. Proverbs 15:30b tells us that "a good report makes the bones healthy". From this verse of Scripture you can see that good reports are good for our health. So, it is important for us to remember the good things the LORD has done for us in the past. Knowing that if HE had done those things for us before, HE is also able to do all those things we are believing HIM for and more. Hallelujah!

In summary, the Apostle Paul encouraged not only the Philippians in Bible days but also us Christians today to meditate on whatsoever things are true, whatsoever things are honest, whatsoever things are just, whatsoever things are pure, whatsoever things are lovely, whatsoever things are of good report and if there be any praise, we should think on these things. We are to deliberately re-set our minds on the things that are positive, pleasant, good, and fix our mind on the Lord Jesus and in His sovereignty over us.

You see, in order for us to let go of the old, the past and the ugly, we are to be transformed by the renewing of our mind and take on the mind of the Lord Jesus. We need to live our lives according to the leading of the Holy Spirit and things of the Spirit (Romans 8:5). We are to consciously leave behind the old man with his old ways and put on the new man in Christ Jesus. For we know that, anyone that is in Christ Jesus is a new creature, old things are passed away, behold all things are become new.

Another method we can adopt for the renewing of our mind, is to speak or confess the word of GOD, which is the word of life. As we continuously and consistently speak the word of GOD to ourselves and family, we will begin to see some transformation in our mind and on the things in which we focus our mind on. In chapter 9 of this book, I have listed some of the scriptures we can confess over ourselves, our family and situations daily.

In Romans 6, we are told to walk in the newness of life after we have been baptised and through the new life that Christ Jesus has given unto us by His death and resurrection. We obtained newness of life when we partake in water baptism by immersion. By us being immersed in the water during water baptism, we bury our old-man with Christ, and we put on the new-man in Christ Jesus when we are raised from the water. Through this ordinance we are identifying ourselves with the Lord Jesus and we are then expected to walk in the newness of life daily.

Romans 6:4 says, "Therefore we are buried with him by baptism into death: that like as Christ was raised up from the dead by the glory of the Father, even so we also should walk in newness of life".

In Ephesians chapter 4, we are told that the spirit of our mind is to be renewed and we are to put on the new man, which is fashioned after GOD in righteousness and true holiness. This is only possible, when we give our life to Jesus Christ of Nazareth and accept Him as our Lord and Saviour. Then, we have to let go of our old ways and embrace our new life in

Christ Jesus through the Holy Spirit, whom we have received when we accepted Christ as our Lord and Saviour. Our lives are renewed from the inside spiritually through the Holy Spirit who dwells in us.

Part of the process of a renewed mind in Christ Jesus is to embrace the fact that, GOD'S love and mercies towards us HIS children are steadfast and are new every morning. HE is a merciful and just FATHER that forgives us when we repent and ask for HIS mercy. HE also wants us to receive from HIM all the benefits HE daily loads us with, so that we can enjoy HIS blessings each and every day.

Lamentations 3:22-23 (ESV) "The steadfast love of the Lord never ceases; his mercies never come to an end; they are new every morning; great is your faithfulness."

THREE
NEW WINE IN THE NEW WINE SKIN

The new wine skin is an empowerment and opportunity the Lord Jesus came to give us, so that we can do away with the old and start afresh and do things better than were done before. He told us in Matthew 9, that we are to put the new wine in new wine skin and not in the old wine skin – in order to profit from the new wine, which He came to give to us through His New Covenant.

When He was addressing the disciples of John the Baptist, He indicated that what He came to do was not going to fit into the system they are used to in the Old Covenant. He came to bring something new that is completely different from what they were used to. He was not implying that the Old Testament was not useful and valuable any longer but that what He came to give them is NEW, which they could not understand. As we know the New Testament completes the Old Testament. Jesus continued by saying to them that, you cannot patch an old garment on a new garment, as that would only make things worse. Therefore, the Lord said to them, the old have to give way for the new. The new cannot be a part of the old because the new comes with much more grace, freedom and liberty.

In the New Covenant, Christ gave us the dispensation of grace and mercy, unlike the Old Testament which was dealing with the Mosaic laws. The New Covenant is written upon our hearts, whilst the Old Testament laws were written on tablet of stones. In the New Testament, we are made a new creature when we give our lives to Christ. The sinner becomes a new creature when he repents of his sins and accepts Christ as his Lord and Saviour. This is not so in the Old Testament. The scriptures tells us in the Old Testament, that the Priest will have to go to the Holy of Holies before the LORD once a year, to make an atonement for the sins of the people, by the sprinkling of the blood of an animal. When Jesus came, He put an end to this, by becoming a sacrifice for us once and for all on the cross of Calvary. Let us examine what the Lord Jesus told us about the new wine in the new wine skin in the gospel:

> "No one sews a piece of new cloth into an old garment, for that which is sewn in to fill it up pulls on the garment, and the tear is made worse. Neither do men put new wine into old wineskins. Or else the wineskins burst, the wine runs out, and the wineskins perish. But they put new wine into new wineskins, and both are preserved."
>
> (MATTHEW 9:16-17)

> "No one sews a piece of new cloth on an old garment, or else the new piece that covered it tears away from the old, and the tear is made worse. And no one pours new wine into old wineskins, or else the new wine bursts the wineskins, and the wine is spilled, and the wineskins will be marred. But new wine must be poured into new wineskins."
>
> (MARK 2:21-22)

"He told them a parable also: 'No one sews a piece of a new material on an old one. Otherwise the new would tear, for the new piece does not match the old. And no one puts new wine into old wineskins. Otherwise the new wine will burst the wineskins, and it will be spilled, and the wineskins will be destroyed. But new wine must be put into new wineskins, and both are preserved. And no one, having drunk old wine, immediately desires new. For he says, "The old is better."'"

(LUKE 5:36-39)

In the account from Luke's gospel 5:36, we are told that the Lord Jesus was speaking in a parable, which means that, this was not given to those with eyes to see and ears to hear but to those who could see and hear and discern things spiritually. Our mortal bodies by nature become old like garments because we are in a fallen world. But the good news is, when we give our lives to Christ and are born again we become a new creation in Him, old things are passed away and all things become new. In Him, we are to put off the old man with his deeds and put on the new man, which is renewed in knowledge after the image of Him that created us. This is part of the mystery of becoming a born again Christian in Christ Jesus. The carnal man cannot understand the things of the Spirit of GOD because they are spiritually discerned.

We need to renew our minds by the power of the Holy Spirit of GOD to receive the good news that the Lord Jesus came to give unto us. In the parable, He told us that the new fabric would be torn if sewn on an old fabric. This He said in reference to the new life He came to give to us. One cannot embrace the new life in Christ and still participate in the old system of worship prior to His coming. He told the Pharisees that cannot be done. You cannot sew a piece of a new cloth in an old one. Because the new would tear as the new piece does not match the old.

The new wine in the new wine skin is likened to the Holy Spirit that the LORD will pour into the new wine skin and the new wine skin is the new man in his immortal body. The Lord Jesus told us in John chapter 3, that we must be born again of water and Spirit to enter into the Kingdom of GOD.

In the days when the Lord Jesus was on earth, wine was kept in wine skins that were made out of animal skins and people at that time were familiar with the art of wine making. They were aware that new wine ferments and increases in volume as gases are formed. New wine skins have the capability to expand and to grow when the wine increases. But the old wine skins are old and wrinkled. They have already been stretched out to full capacity and cannot expand any further. When they are filled out they will not have space for the gases and they will break and the wine will leak. Therefore, if you put new wine into an old wine skin it will burst because it does not have any elasticity to expand any further. If you pour new wine in an old wine skin, you would waste both the new wine and the old wine skin. Why did the Lord Jesus tell us this parable? He was explaining to the Pharisees that the NEW life he came to give them will not fit into the old system they are used to. He was telling them that there is going to be a change because GOD is doing a NEW thing. No more animal sacrifice, for HE Christ is going to be the sacrifice for all mankind once and forever.

For He said, "I am come that they might have life, and have it more abundantly" (John 10:10b). Not life like they knew it and it is going to be a NEW life in Him. But the Pharisees could not comprehend what the Master was saying because they were like the old wine skin, that is stiff and impermeable that cannot be stretched any further or they will burst and leak out their contents.

This is why it is necessary for us to have a renewed mind in Christ to contain the fresh out pouring of the Holy Spirit. For our faith increases as we grow in the word of GOD. We are to put on the mind of Christ, which is always connected to the LORD. The mind of Christ, is the mind that is always ready to do the will of GOD the FATHER and it is a new mind that can be stretched without bursting because it is renewed daily by the precious Holy Spirit of GOD.

We need to put new wine in the new wine skin that is fresh and able to preserve the new wine. We need new strategies for the new season the Lord has brought us into. We need to renew our minds daily with the word of GOD. We need to stop the old sinful ways of doing things and embrace GOD'S ways of doing things. With the new comes grace, freedom, rest, favour, fruitfulness, joy, strength, opportunities and so much more. But in order to flow into the new, we need to let go of the old and of yesterday, to make room for the new in our lives.

The Lord is saying it is time for us to put the new wine in the new wine skin. It is time to embrace all the free gifts of salvation He came to give unto us through His New Covenant of grace. It is time for us to drop the old ways of doing things and start walking in the newness of life, new ways of thinking, new and better ways of relating to our families, loved ones and friends. This is especially true, if the old ways of doing things were not profitable. We must do away with the old wine skin for the new wine skin. It is time to give our life to Christ, forgive others and let go of offences and bitterness. We must ensure we do not put new wine in the old wine skin but in the new wine skin, so that we can produce much fruits in our lives and achieve greatly in our day to day walk with the LORD than ever before.

In order for us to enjoy this new era we are in now, things have to change. They cannot remain the same. This is the time to allow the LORD to rearrange things in our lives and move things away from our lives that should not be there in the first place. We need to be flexible in the hands of the LORD, for HE is the Potter and we are the clay. I believe in this new season, the hand of GOD is shifting and redefining things in the lives of HIS people and the only thing we have to do is to yield to HIM as HE realigns us to HIS plan for us in this season. The

IT'S A NEW SEASON

Lord Jesus came to redefine the script. So that whosoever that believe in Him will not perish but will be saved and have everlasting life. He came to do a new thing in the lives of mankind and move us into things that look unfamiliar to what has been and what was.

We need to let go of the familiar, our comfort zone, traditions, things and people that cannot go with us into the NEW place GOD is taking us into. We need to let go of the past to embrace the new. We need to let go of the old-wine-skin. We need to do away with the old ways of doing things and follow the ways and directions of the LORD. So that we will obtain all that HE has for us and fulfil HIS purpose for us on this earth.

We should not continue with the old wine skin as the Lord is telling us to let go of it. Do not resist the new wine skin by attempting to hold on to what was, or what we are used to or comfortable with because of fear and uncertainty. We need to trust GOD and follow HIM wherever HE may be taking us or leading us to, for HE knows better than us. Let us hold on to HIS hand and not let go of it. Take the hand of the LORD and trust HIM, for there is a glorious new season rising. For we know that the plans HE has towards us, are of peace and for our well-being and not of evil, to give us a future and expected end.

Often, when we are going through change we go through a process. To go through a transition from the old to the new takes time and it can be difficult. But we need to allow the LORD to take us through the process of change to benefit from the change. We need to yield to the Holy Spirit of GOD as we embrace the change and not delay the process by holding on to the old wine skins. It is time to change the old wine skins for the new wine skins. So that we do not waste the new wine the Lord is pouring upon us. The new wine skins are upon us, can you not tell? Everything is changing around us and we need to move in synchronization with the Lord's agenda. Because this new wine cannot be wasted. It is too precious to be wasted. It is a new era, a new season and things are becoming totally different from what they have been.

The Coronavirus pandemic has forced a lot of institutions all around the world to start doing things differently. It is time to say goodbye to the old ways of doing things and adapt to the change in order to make progress. Many things will not be the same. This means that the familiar and the old normal are gradually fading away because the new normal is upon us. The new methods of doing things are to be enhanced, embraced and maximized, for change has come to stay.

In Ephesians chapter 4, we are told to put off the old man concerning the previous conversation, which is corrupt according to the deceitful lusts. It continues to say we should be renewed in the spirit of our mind and put on the new (regenerated) man, which is created in righteousness and holiness of the truth in the image of GOD.

Ephesians 4:22-24 says, "That ye put off concerning the former conversation the old man, which is corrupt according to the deceitful lusts; And be renewed in the spirit of your mind; And that ye put on the new man, which after God is created in righteousness and true holiness."

Amongst others, here are some of the things we need to put off to help us to truly prosper and flourish in the new man in Christ Jesus:

1. We should put off untruthfulness. We should speak the truth to our neighbour for we are members of one of another (Ephesians 4:25).

2. We should put off grudges, anger, malice and bitterness. We should not give the enemy an occasion to lead us into sin by holding grudges, nurturing anger or harbouring resentment or cultivating bitterness (Ephesians 4:27).
3. We should put off stealing. We should not take that which is not ours. The person that use to steal should cease from stealing but rather work hard in making an honest living, producing that which is good with his own hands, so that he will be a blessing to the needy (Ephesians 4:28).
4. We should put off corrupt and profane communications. We should be mindful of our words and not let no corrupt, foul, profane, worthless, and vulgar words come out of our mouth but that which is good to the use of edifying, that it may minister grace unto the hearers (Ephesians 4:29).
5. We should not grieve the Holy Spirit of GOD. We are not to grieve the Holy Spirit of GOD but we should seek to please Him, by whom we are sealed unto the day of redemption (Ephesians 4:30).
6. We should put off our old self. We should

completely put away from us bitterness, wrath, anger, perpetual animosity and evil speaking, also with every kind of malice (Ephesians 4:31).

There are other things that can help us to do away with the old man so that we can enjoy the new man and new wine skin the Lord Jesus came to give us. We can be kind, helpful to one another and be tender hearted and forgive one another just as GOD for Christ's sake also forgave us (Ephesians 4:32).

Furthermore, we are told in the book of Colossians, to be truthful, seeing that we have put off the old man with his deeds. We should put on the new man, which is renewed in knowledge after the image of Him that created us:

> "Lie not one to another, seeing that ye have put off the old man with his deeds; And have put on the new man, which is renewed in knowledge after the image of him that created him."
>
> (COLOSSIANS 3:9-10)

Here is the Amplified Bible's version of the same scripture:

> "Do not lie to one another, for you have stripped off the old self with its evil practices, and have put on the new [spiritual] self who is being continually renewed in true knowledge in the image of Him who created the new self."
>
> (COLOSSIANS 3:9-10)

In the Amplified Bible, we are told to strip off the old self with its evil practices and we are to put on the new spiritual self who is continually renewed in the true knowledge of GOD who created us.

From the above scriptures, we can see how the word of GOD encourages the born again Christian, to do away with the sinful nature of the former self and its deeds and to put on the new man that is regenerated and renewed by the Holy Spirit every day. The new wineskins are upon us and we need His glorious new wine in this new season. We are to drink the new wine from the new wine skins and be excited about it. We need to embrace the unfamiliar, knowing that He is with us always. We are to walk in sync with Him as he takes us to His fountain of life, to the well of life, to drink of His love and mercy in this new season. Let us be obedient to His voice, as He reveals His glory to us in this new season. So that we can enjoy the New Wine which flows from His everlasting fountain and that never runs dry. The Lord Jesus is pouring upon us (His vessels) the new wine freely to enjoy and to serve Him through His New Covenant of Grace. Let us drink from the new wine skins through the precious Holy Spirit of GOD.

FOUR

MINISTRY OF ANGELS IN THE NEW SEASON

I believe strongly that in this new season we are to engage with the angels of GOD more than we have ever done before to expedite the fulfilment of our assignments on planet earth. More especially, the body of Christ needs to work with the angels GOD has assigned to the church in order to advance HIS Kingdom. I would like to start this chapter by looking at some of the things the Bible tells us about the angels of GOD.

In Psalm 103, we are told that the angels of GOD excel in strength, they execute the commandments of the LORD, they obey the voice of the LORD, they are the hosts of heaven that execute the pleasures of the LORD, they are spiritual personalities and they are real. They also carry out decrees of the children of GOD to bring them to pass and enforce the power of the Kingdom of GOD.

Angels are magnificent beings that have the released energy of GOD'S power. In the scriptures they are referred to as holy and mighty angels. They carry the assignment of the Holy Spirit. They are ministering spirit that GOD has commissioned to minister to those who will inherit salvation. And they are not to be worshipped (Colossians 2:18).

They are invincible and we cannot touch them but they can touch us and protect us. In Psalm 91, the Scripture tells us that the LORD has given HIS angels authority to protect us wherever we may go. They will carry us in their mighty hands, so that we do not stumble or fall:

> "For he shall give his angels charge over thee, to keep thee in all thy ways. They shall bear thee up in their hands, lest thou dash thy foot against a stone."
>
> (PSALM 91:11-12)

Let us now look at the part the angelic hosts played in the ministry of the Lord Jesus when He was here on earth. As we are told in the gospel it was an angel of the LORD that announced His coming to the virgin Mary.

The Announcement of the Lord Jesus' Conception

We are told in the book of Luke chapter 1, that angel Gabriel was sent from GOD to Mary, a virgin in a city of Galilee called Nazareth. He informed her that she was blessed among women and highly favoured by GOD and that she was going to conceive in her womb and bring forth a son. His name will be Jesus, He shall be great and shall be called the Son of the Highest. He shall rule over the house of Jacob forever and there shall be no end to His Kingdom:

> "And in the sixth month the angel Gabriel was sent from God unto a city of Galilee, named Nazareth. To a virgin espoused to a man whose name was Joseph, of the house of David; and the virgin's name was Mary. And the angel came in unto her, and said, Hail, thou that art highly favoured, the Lord is with thee: blessed art thou among women. And when she saw him, she was troubled at his saying, and cast in her mind what manner of salutation this should be. And the angel said unto her, Fear not,

Mary: for thou hast found favour with God. And, behold, thou shalt conceive in thy womb, and bring forth a son, and shalt call his name Jesus. He shall be great, and shall be called the Son of the Highest: and the Lord God shall give unto him the throne of his father David: And he shall reign over the house of Jacob for ever; and of his kingdom there shall be no end."

(LUKE 1:26-33)

The Announcement of Birth of the Lord Jesus

After the birth of the Lord Jesus, an angel of the LORD announced His birth to the shepherds camping in the field of Bethlehem who were, watching over their flocks at night. The Scriptures also tells us that the glory of the LORD surrounded them. The angel of the LORD, informed them that he has brought good news of great joy to them and for the whole world. The angel continued by saying that a Saviour has been born unto them in the city of David, which is Christ the Lord. He gave them a sign of how baby Jesus would be found. So that when they did find Him they would be able to identify Him. He said that, the baby would be wrapped in swaddling clothes and lying in a manger. After the angel had delivered his message to the shepherds that night he was suddenly joined by a host of angels from heaven praising GOD:

"And Joseph also went up from Galilee, out of the city of Nazareth, into Judaea, unto the city of David, which is called Bethlehem; (because he was of the house and lineage of David:). To be taxed with Mary his espoused wife, being great with child. And so it was, that, while they were there, the days were accomplished that she should be delivered. And she brought forth her firstborn son, and wrapped him in swaddling clothes, and laid him in a manger; because there was no room for them in the inn. And there were in the same country shepherds abiding in the field, keeping watch over their flock by night. And, lo, the angel of the Lord came upon them, and the glory of the Lord shone round about them: and they were sore afraid. And the angel said unto them, Fear not: for, behold, I bring you good tidings of great joy, which shall be to all people. For unto you is born this day in the city of David a Saviour, which is Christ the Lord. And this shall be a sign unto you; Ye shall find the babe wrapped in swaddling clothes, lying in a manger. And suddenly there was with the angel a multitude of the heavenly host praising God, and saying, Glory to God in the highest, and on earth peace, good will toward men. And it came to pass, as the angels were gone away from them into heaven, the shepherds said one to another, Let us now go even unto Bethlehem, and see this thing which is come to pass, which the Lord hath made known unto us. And they came with haste, and found Mary, and Joseph, and the babe lying in a manger."

(LUKE 2:4-12)

After the Birth of the Lord Jesus

After the birth of the Lord Jesus, an angel of the LORD appeared to Joseph in a dream to warn him about the intention of king Herod to kill the baby. The angel instructed Joseph to leave Bethlehem with both Mary and baby Jesus and depart to Egypt. He asked Joseph to stay in Egypt until he had been told of the way forward of their journey. They stayed in Egypt until the death of Herod. When king Herod died, the angel of the LORD appeared again to Joseph in Egypt in a dream and asked him to depart with Mary and the baby to Israel. We see an account of this in the book of Matthew 2:8–23.

Also, when the Lord Jesus was tempted by the devil after He had fasted for forty days and forty nights, we are told in Matthew chapter 4 that the angels of the LORD came and ministered to Him.

The Lord Jesus' Resurrection

After His death on the cross at Calvary, the Lord Jesus' body was taken down from the cross and buried in a new garden sepulchre. On the third day, Mary Magdalene went very early to the sepulchre when it was still dark and realised that the stone had been rolled away where they had buried Him and His body was no longer there. As she stood there crying, she stooped down and looked into the tomb, and there she saw two angels in white sitting, one at the head and the other at the feet where the body of the Lord Jesus was laid. When they asked her why she was crying, she said to them that they had taken away the body of her Lord and she did not know where they had taken it to. Little did she know that the Lord Jesus had already been resurrected as He said He would on the third day:

"The first day of the week cometh Mary Magdalene early, when it was yet dark, unto the sepulchre, and seeth the stone taken away from the sepulchre. But Mary stood without at the sepulchre weeping: and as she wept, she stooped down, and looked into the sepulchre, And seeth two angels in white sitting, the one at the head, and the other at the feet, where the body of Jesus had lain. And they say unto her, Woman, why weepest thou? She saith unto them, Because they have taken away my Lord, and I know not where they have laid him. And when she had thus said, she turned herself back, and saw Jesus standing, and knew not that it was Jesus."

(MATTHEW 20:1, 11-14)

The Lord Jesus' Ascension

We are told in the book of Acts chapter 1 that, after the Lord Jesus had ascended into heaven, two men in white robes appeared to the disciples and said to them, "Men of Galilee, why are you looking toward heaven?" And they continued by saying, "This same Jesus that you have seen going to heaven shall come again to the earth in the same way you have seen Him go." I believe these were not ordinary men robed in white but these were the angels of GOD, comforting the men of Galilee.

We can see clearly from the above instances how the angels of the LORD supported the Ministry of the Lord Jesus Christ when He was here on earth. My question to you then is this: if the Lord Jesus who is the Son of the Most High GOD, the one that knew no sin needed the services of the angelic hosts, then what would you say about you and me? Don't you think that we, as well, need their support to accomplish our GOD-given assignment here on earth? I believe we too as children of GOD would require their supernatural support, especially now more than ever before, in this new era. And because the Lord Jesus' coming is imminent, we need the angelic hosts to help us fulfil our purpose here on earth before the Lord's return.

The Purpose of the Angels of GOD

Have you ever thought about the purpose of angels and why GOD created them? We are told in the scriptures that they are messengers of GOD. They have been assigned to us to help us to fulfil our purpose here on earth.

The Almighty GOD assigned HIS Angel to Moses and the children of Israel when they were leaving Egypt to protect and lead them into their prepared place, the Promised Land. The LORD said to them, that they should be cautious when they are before Him, they should listen to Him, they should be obedient to Him and they should not arouse Him, for HE will not forgive their offence if they provoked Him. He said that because HIS authority is upon this Angel. The LORD also told them if they listened and obeyed this Angel HE had assigned to assist them, then HE GOD Almighty will be an enemy to their enemies and an adversary to their adversaries.

Why was it important for the children of Israel to cooperate with this Angel of GOD and obey Him? I would like to believe it was because this particular Angel was no other but the Lord Jesus Christ the Son of GOD, who is able to forgive sins. That is why the LORD said that if the children of Israel were disobedient to Him or provoked Him, He would not pardon their transgressions since HIS name is in Him. Christ was the Angel of GOD that went before the children of Israel, carried them day and night, protected them and saved them through the wilderness. GOD promised the children of Israel that,

IT'S A NEW SEASON

when HIS Angel goes before them and brings them before their enemies, HE will give them victory and bring them into the Promised Land:

> "Behold, I am going to send an Angel before you to keep and guard you on the way and to bring you to the place I have prepared. Be on your guard before Him, to listen to and obey His voice; do not be rebellious toward Him or provoke Him, for He will not pardon your transgression, since My Name (authority) is in Him. But if you will indeed listen to and truly obey His voice and do everything that I say, then I will be an enemy to your enemies and an adversary to your adversaries. When My Angel goes before you and brings you to [the land of] the Amorite, the Hittite, the Perizzite, the Canaanite, the Hivite, and the Jebusite, I will reject them and completely destroy them."
>
> (EXODUS 23:20-23) [AMP]

Just like the LORD assigned HIS angel to Moses and the children of Israel in the Old Testament to support them in accomplishing their mission through the desert and brought them into the Promised Land, so HE has also assigned HIS angelic hosts to help us in the pursuit and fulfilment of our destinies. They were created to serve and worship the Almighty GOD and also to serve mankind. The LORD loved us so much that HE created these powerful majestic beings to serve and to minister to us. He has assigned them to us to ensure that HIS plans for each of us HIS children are fulfilled. In Jeremiah chapter 29, the LORD says that HIS plans for us are good and not evil, to give us a hope and an expected end, as it is written in our book in heaven. I strongly believe that we can unravel what the LORD has written in our book in heaven and accomplish our assignments, by engaging with our angels He has assigned to us to help us fulfil our purpose and expected end. One of their purposes is to also activate us to read our books and accomplish here on earth what is written in them in heaven as stated in the book of Psalms:

"My frame was not hidden from You,

When I was being formed in secret,

And intricately and skillfully formed [as if embroidered with many colors] in the depths of the earth. Your eyes have seen my unformed substance;

And in Your book were all written the days that were appointed for me,

When as yet there was not one of them [even taking shape]."

(PSALM 139:15-16) [AB]

In verse 16 of Psalm 139, we can see that everything the LORD GOD Almighty wants us to fulfil here on earth has already been designed or written for us in our books in heaven. Isn't our GOD an awesome GOD? No wonder HE is called the Alpha and Omega, the beginning and the end in the book of Revelation. HE is truly the Author and the Finisher of our faith. HE already knows our end from our beginning. Therefore, HE has assigned to us angelic support to help us execute what is written in our books in heaven here on earth. The angels of GOD are around us to make sure that the word of GOD is activated in our lives. They go on to perform what GOD has said about us and ensure that it bears much fruit in us.

We need angelic support in this new season to conquer and to be victorious. For it is the will of GOD for us to accomplish our purpose on earth. For us to be able to do so we will have to partner with our angels on assignment. Through prayers and divine revelation, GOD will mobilise HIS angels to support us in our work with HIM. The angels of GOD are not only around to protect us as written in Psalm 91, that HE shall give HIS angels charge over us to keep us in all our ways, but they are also around us to help us fulfil GOD's plans for our lives.

Job 22:28 tells us that, we shall also decree a thing and it shall be established unto us and the light of GOD shall shine upon our ways. I strongly believe that when we decree a thing, the angels of GOD respond to the word that was decreed and bring it to pass. In other words, we are releasing an assignment to the angels when we decree a thing. So you can see that, the LORD has released them unto us to help us accomplish our purpose on earth. In this new era we are in, to be victorious, we will have to engage our angels that have been assigned to us by GOD, by speaking GOD'S words over our lives and families daily, for they listen to the words of the King of kings and execute them.

We do not only engage and activate our angels when we make a decree, but also when we pray. They bring answers to our prayers when we pray. In the book of Daniel, we are told that an angel of GOD was sent to him by the LORD, to bring answers to his prayers:

> "Then behold, a hand touched me and set me unsteadily on my hands and knees. So he said to me, 'O Daniel, you highly regarded and greatly beloved man, understand the words that I am about to say to you and stand upright, for I have now been sent to you.' And while he was saying this word to me, I stood up trembling. Then he said to me, 'Do not be afraid, Daniel, for from the first day that you set your heart on understanding this and on humbling yourself before your God, your words were heard, and I have come in response to your words.'"
>
> (DANIEL 10:10-12)

Engaging our Angels

As we can see from the above scriptures we have looked at, GOD has assigned angels to help us achieve and accomplish our GOD given purpose for our lives. So, we have a part to play by cooperating with them at all times. We need to engage with them and not to leave them idle.

We can engage with our angels by decreeing GOD'S word aloud in our lives daily.

The Spirit of GOD is upon HIS word, so when we decree and declare HIS words upon our lives and situations, we are engaging the angels of GOD to execute them as we have said and bring them to pass. In John chapter 6, the Lord Jesus told us that the words that HE speaks are spirit and they are life. Then, it is imperative that we are mindful of our words at all times because our angels, even though they are invisible to our physical realm, are always around us to execute our declarations.

Do not leave your angels unemployed by not cooperating with them. But engage them by consistently declaring GOD's word over your life, your children's life, your husband's life, your marriage, your ministry, your business, your career and so on. After you have made these declarations of GOD'S word over your lives, watch and see how the LORD uses HIS angels to bring them to pass in your lives. One thing we need to know is that we do not have to see the angels of GOD like those who have been gifted by GOD to see angels for them to execute our prayers and declarations for us. For GOD has

IT'S A NEW SEASON

made them ministering spirits, assigned by HIM to minister to us HIS children.

I believe that when we pray in the spirit, we are also engaging our angels who understand our spiritual languages and activate them to harken to what we are saying in the spiritual realm. This can be very powerful, especially when we are praying in the spirit with understanding. There is power and revelation when we pray in the spirit. We can engage our angels when we are worshipping the Lord, for they themselves also worship the Lamb of GOD as we are told in Hebrews chapter 5.

What more can we learn about the angels of GOD from the scriptures?

They Exhibit Power

In chapter 28 of Matthew's account of the Lord's resurrection we are told that, when the Lord Jesus was buried on the third day there was a great earthquake, and an angel of the LORD descended from heaven and rolled away the stone from the door of the sepulchre where the Lord Jesus was buried and sat upon it. This act of the angel demonstrated power, which makes me believe that they are heavenly beings with great power.

They are Messengers of GOD

They bring messages from GOD to HIS children. Angel Gabriel was sent to Zacharias the priest, whilst he was burning incense in the temple of the LORD. He announced to him that GOD has answered his prayer and his wife Elizabeth was going to bear a son and his name shall be called John, "He shall be great in the sight of the LORD and will drink neither wine nor strong drink and shall be filled with the Holy Ghost even in his mother's womb. Because of him, many of the children of Israel shall return to the LORD their GOD" (Luke 1:15-16).

In the same chapter of Luke, the angel Gabriel was also sent by the LORD to Mary, to tell her that she has been favoured and chosen amongst women by HIM, to be the mother of the Saviour of the world, the Lord Jesus.

When the Apostle Paul was on a shipwreck on his way to Italy to be tried by Caesar, an angel of GOD appeared to him in the night and encouraged him not to be afraid. He also affirmed to him that no one on board the ship will perish but they will all make it to the shore alive (Acts 23:23–25).

They are our Spiritual Bodyguards that Protect Us

The LORD has assured us, HIS children, that no evil shall befall us, neither shall any plague come near our dwelling place because, HE the LORD GOD Almighty, has given HIS angels (notice plural) charge over us to keep us in all our ways. That is not all, they (the angels) shall also carry us up in their strong and mighty hands, so that we do not hit our feet against stones and injure ourselves or fall (Psalm 91:10–12). This is amazing! In these verses, we can see the love our heavenly FATHER has for us. Hallelujah! It is a true privilege to be loved and cared for by our heavenly FATHER.

When an allegation was made against Daniel and he was thrown into the den of lions, the LORD Almighty sent HIS angel to shut the mouth of the lions, so that they would not eat him up or hurt him. As we know, lions are carnivorous animals and would have eaten Daniel alive, if the LORD had not sent HIS mighty angel to close their mouths in the den. We should be comforted too, that the LORD has assigned them to protect us at all times. Praise the LORD!

They Bring us Deliverance

They are GOD'S mighty warriors that bring us deliverance from our enemies and troubles. The LORD sent an angel to Gideon to deliver the children of Israel out of the hands of the Midianites. While Gideon was hiding in a winepress from the Midianites, separating some wheat from the chaff, an angel of the LORD came to Ophrah and sat down under an oak tree belonging to Gideon's father, Joash the Abi-ezrite. The angel appeared unto Gideon and said to him, "The LORD is with you, mighty warrior!" Also, in the same chapter we are told, the LORD in the form of an angel, said to him, "Go with your strength and save Israel from the Midianites: have not I sent thee?" Since Gideon had that encounter with the Angel of the LORD, he was delivered from the intimidation and fear of the enemies that threatened his nation Israel at that time. Also, his destiny was restored by the encounter he had with the Angel of the LORD (Judges 6:12-14).

In the New Testament, we see how the angels of the LORD were sent by GOD to deliver Peter, Paul and Silas from prison. In the Old Testament, we are told of how the LORD delivered the children of Israel from the Assyrians by just one angel. The warrior angel of the LORD was sent to fight for the children of Israel and killed 185,000 people in one night (2 Kings 19:35). Hallelujah!

I pray that the LORD GOD Almighty, will send HIS angels to fight your enemies today, in the Mighty name of Jesus.

These activities of the angels of GOD, demonstrates the supernatural powers they possess to deliver us from troubles.

We have seen the part they played in supporting the ministry of the Lord Jesus here on earth, during His birth, death and resurrection. The LORD commissions them to bring us revelation of what is written in our books in heaven and also help us in accomplishing them. In Psalm 139 we are told, all the days the LORD has planned for each and every one of us are written in our books in heaven, even before we were formed in our mothers' womb. Just as they supported the Lord Jesus' ministry whilst He was here on earth, so has the LORD assigned them to us, to help us to fulfil our GOD given destinies as written in our books in heaven. I strongly believe that we will not be able to accomplish our GOD given purposes here on earth without the help of the Holy Spirit and the assistance of the angels of GOD.

They are not to be Worshipped

As we have already read, the angels of GOD are heavenly beings that worship GOD and execute HIS commands. In the book of Revelation, this is what John the Revelator was told when he fell down to worship the angel who was with him:

> "Then saith he unto me, See thou do it not: for I am thy fellowservant, and of thy brethren the prophets, and of them which keep the sayings of this book: worship God."
>
> (REVELATION 22:9)

As we can see from the above scripture, we are not to worship them for they are our fellow servants but we are to worship GOD and HIM alone must we worship.

They Bring Answers and the Manifestation of Miracles to our Prayers

In Daniel chapter 10, we are told that Daniel prayed to GOD regarding a vision he had about a great war to come. He understood the vision and its message and was greatly disturbed about it. So, he decided to seek the face of the LORD for HIS guidance into the matter and the LORD answered his prayers immediately. However, he could not receive the manifestation of his prayers at the time they were answered by GOD. Because the prince of the kingdom of Persia tried to stop the angel of GOD for twenty-one days, from delivering the answers to Daniel's prayers until angel Michael, one of the most prominent angels, was sent to support him from being delayed any further by the enemy.

We can see from Daniel's situation how the angelic hosts help us to receive the manifestation of answered prayers, even when the enemy tries to stop them from coming to pass. This is just awesome!

In this new season, we need more angelic assistance to help us accomplish our assignments and to fulfil the great commission given unto us believers by the Lord Jesus, especially when His second coming is fast approaching. The good news is that, they that be for us are greater than those who are against us (2 Kings 6:16).

The LORD and HIS angelic hosts are on our side, working on our behalf daily. So, we need to focus on the LORD more and more each day and HIS agenda for our lives. For we know, HE is the Author and the Finisher of our faith. HE has given HIS legion of angels charge over us to support and keep us in all our ways. Glory be to a GOD!

FIVE
MADE NEW BY THE BLOOD OF JESUS

Jesus came to the earth from His throne in heaven to give us a new and better covenant through His precious blood. His coming to this earth moved mankind from the old into the new dispensation of grace. From the Old Covenant of the Law written on the tablet of stones to the New Covenant of Grace written on our hearts. The blood He shed for us on the Cross at Calvary, is the blood of the New Covenant which He shed for many for the remission of sin. Without the shedding of blood, there is no remission of sins and without the remission of sin there is no life. By the shedding of His blood, the Lord Jesus obtained a new life for us. He shed His blood for us, to reconcile us back to our GOD and to give us direct access to HIS throne room. He took our sins upon Himself, in order that we will be forgiven by GOD and have the opportunity again to start a new and better life with HIM. The precious blood of Jesus was the perfect covering of our sins, so that we will be made righteous through the shedding of His blood. We have been washed from our old sinful nature and made new into a new man by the precious blood of Jesus.

Through the precious blood of Jesus, as born again Christians and believers in the Lord Jesus the Messiah, we have been redeemed back to our GOD after the fall of Adam at the garden of Eden. We have not only been redeemed back to our GOD but we have also been made kings and priests unto our GOD to rule and reign in the earth (Revelation 5:9–10).

There is power in the blood of Jesus, to not only wash away our sins but also to make us new. His blood has cleansed us from all sins and translated us from darkness into His marvellous light. We have been made white as snow by the precious Blood of Jesus. Revelation chapter 7, tells us that the blood of the Lamb has washed the robes of those who came out of the great tribulation and made them white. Hallelujah! There is power in the blood of the Lamb to cleanse us from our unrighteousness and from all sins.

We have not only been made new through the blood of Jesus but we have now been clothed with the robe of righteousness. The Lord Jesus who knew no sin was made sin for us, so that we might be made the righteousness of GOD in Him. By His blood, the Lord Jesus obtained for us a more excellent ministry, by how much also He is the mediator of a better and new covenant, which was established upon better promises (Hebrews 8:6).

The Lord through His blood has freed us from our old and sinful lifestyle into a new life in Him by washing away our sins. Also, by His own blood has made us his people, who were once unholy, holy. So that we can come boldly into the throne room of GOD to obtain mercy and grace in time of need. The Lord Jesus' blood that He shed for us on the Cross at Calvary, did not just wash away our sins and bring us into a New Covenant with our GOD, it also has an inexhaustible power to preserve us from harm and danger. The blood of Jesus is the Christian's comprehensive insurance and assurance.

During the Passover in Egypt, the LORD told Moses that at midnight HE will go out into the midst of the Egyptians and all the first born of Egypt will die. From Pharaoh's firstborn who sits upon his throne, unto the firstborn that is behind the mill and all firstborn of beasts. This is because Pharaoh, their king, refused to let the children of Israel go to serve HIM, their GOD and maker. But amongst the children of Israel, all firstborns of both man and beast were spared and preserved. In order for the firstborn of the children of Israel to be preserved, every household was required to kill a male unblemished lamb of the first year and use the blood and strike it on the two side posts and on the upper doorpost of the house, where they will eat the lamb. So that when the LORD sees the blood on their doorposts, HE will pass over them without destroying the firstborn of that family and they would be exempted from the plague of the land. The lamb was a substitute for the Israelites' firstborn sons. The blood of the lamb on their doorposts was a clear reminder of the price that was paid for them, so that the life of their firstborns could be saved.

If the blood of a lamb could be used to preserve the life of the children of Israel, how much more the blood of Jesus? His blood has preserved us from the punishment of sin that was committed at the garden of Eden, by Adam and Eve. The Lord Jesus is the Son of GOD, who left His throne in heaven and came down to earth to die for mankind. Imagine what His blood would do for us who believe in Him. He shed His blood for us on the Cross at Calvary to transition us from the Old Covenant of the Law written on the tablet of stones to the New Covenant of Grace written on our hearts. Hallelujah!

By the power in His precious blood, the Lord Jesus has made us brand new and restored us back to our GOD. He took away our sins, our former carnal nature, sicknesses, diseases, the evil reports of enemy against us, poverty, shame, disgrace, limitations, accusations and so many other things that were against us, and nailed them ALL on to the cross and said, "It is finished." He did this so that, we may be restored back to our heavenly FATHER. He died for us on the cross that we might have life and have it more abundantly.

When we were dead in our sins and in the uncircumcision of our flesh, the worldliness of our former lifestyle, GOD made us alive together with Christ. HE freely forgave us of all our sins, by cancelling out with His blood the certificate of debt consisting of legal demands, which were in force against us and which were hostile to us. And this certificate the Lord Jesus put aside and completely removed by nailing it to the cross. When He had disarmed the rulers and authorities, those supernatural forces of evil operating against us, He made a public example of them by exhibiting them as captives in His triumphal procession, having triumphed over them through the cross. The Lord Jesus Christ of Nazareth, won the victory for us on the cross, that we may have a new life in Him. 2 Corinthians chapter 5 tells us, if any man be in Christ, he is a new creation, and old things are passed away, behold all things have become new.

I believe strongly that we cannot embrace the new life that the Lord Jesus obtained for us on the cross by shedding his precious blood, if we do not let go of the past that has weighed us down. It is time to do away with all that has held us back from enjoying the benefits of the cross. We need to take off the old man with his sinful nature and lustful deeds and put on the new man. Which is renewed in knowledge after the image of HIM that created us. We are also told in Romans chapter 13, to put on the Lord Jesus Christ and make no provision for the flesh to fulfil its lusts.

We are to put on the Lord, so that we can walk in holiness and righteousness of the truth at all times. Our Lord and Saviour Jesus Christ, gave Himself for us that He might redeem us from all iniquity, and purify unto Himself a peculiar people that are zealous of all good works. As we embrace the Lord Jesus and all He has done for us through His precious blood, the Holy Spirit of GOD will come and dwell in us, rest upon us and empower us to be all that GOD has ordained for us in HIS Kingdom in this new season. Hallelujah!

SIX
DIVINE RECOVERY IN THE NEW SEASON

We cannot talk about divine recovery without talking about the redemptive work the Lord Jesus did for us on the cross at Calvary through His blood. Jesus died to recover us from our sin and reconcile us back to our GOD. Because of the fall of man at the Garden of Eden, we needed to be redeemed back to our GOD. HE had a plan to redeem us back to HIMSELF, by sending HIS only begotten Son to die for ALL mankind by shedding His blood at Calvary to bring us back to HIMSELF. It is my belief that just like the LORD sent Christ Jesus to redeem us back to HIMSELF, so is HIS desire for us HIS children to recover back ALL that the enemy has stolen from us since we were in our mother's womb. Because HIS redemption is an act of divine recovery and restoration of mankind back to his original state, plan and purpose, as HE had ordained it to be even from the beginning of time.

The LORD has brought you and me into our new season to bless us and empower us to recover all that the enemy has stolen from us and all we have lost. The Scripture tells us that when a thief is caught he must pay back sevenfold and must give back all the wealth in his house (Proverbs 6:31). This is our time to recover back sevenfold and more all the enemy has stolen from us. Regardless of when the goods were stolen or the theft and damage was done, it is time to recover all. The time has come to seek GOD our heavenly FATHER'S face for supernatural strategies to recover all our fortunes and all that the enemy has stolen from us. It is only GOD that knows where the enemy has taken the things he has stolen from us HIS children. HE is able to guide us and show us where they have been kept and give us divine recovery strategies and angelic support to recover all. Hallelujah!

The word recovery means to "retake, to take back, regain (anything or health), become well, restore to consciousness, to snatch away, pluck away, to restore, to recover, to live, to revive, return to soberness or to do well". (International Standard Bible Encyclopaedia).

As we can see from the above list of meanings of the word recovery, we can deduce that it is a positive and inspiring word. It is a word that tells us there is a way out, there is hope and there is another opportunity. It also reminds us that all is not lost, for our GOD is a GOD of a second chance, a third chance and many other chances and HE is merciful to give us many more opportunities again. In other words, the word "recovery" is a word of encouragement assuring us that if GOD made it happened before, HE is able to make it happen again.

The word recovery is a noun that stemmed from the word "to recover" a verb. As we know, a verb is an action word. To recover all that the enemy has stolen from us, we need to fold up our sleeves and take some actions. One of the definitions of the word recover listed above is to "pluck away". It is time to pluck back what is rightfully ours from the hands of the enemy. The Lord Jesus told us in Matthew chapter 11, that from the days of John the Baptist until now, the kingdom of heaven suffers violence and the violent takes it back by force. We need to be more aggressive to recover all our stolen goods from the enemy's camp. We need to reposition ourselves to snatch back from the enemy what he stole from us and what is rightfully ours.

It is time to pray until something happens (P.U.S.H). It is also that time to seek the face of our GOD again in fasting and praying for divine recovery strategies. As we wait on HIM we need to reposition ourselves for divine direction for divine recovery. It is time to recover our goods, our health, our strength, our finances, our relationships, our careers, our businesses, our marriages, our family, our children or whatsoever it may be for you, back from the hands of the enemy.

Our heavenly FATHER is a Righteous Judge (Psalm 7:11; 1 Peter 1:17). He does not like injustice and HE certainly does not like it when HIS children are being taken advantage of. When we come to HIM and pour out our hearts to HIM in prayer, HE is always ready to help us regardless of the gravity of the matter. When the children of Israel were being taken as slaves in Egypt, they cried unto the GOD of Israel, the Strength of Israel and HE heard their cries. He said unto Moses, 'I have seen the affliction MY people have suffered in Egypt and I have heard their cries as a result of the wickedness of their taskmasters. I am concerned about their suffering and I have come down to deliver them from the Egyptians' (Exodus 3:7—8a). He sent help for them through Moses to deliver them from their hard labour, freed them from slavery and the wickedness of the Egyptians after 430 years in Egypt. The LORD delivered the children of Israel from bondage and brought them to the Promised Land, a good land flowing with milk and honey. But HE did not allow them to leave Egypt empty, for they needed to recover back all that Pharaoh and the Egyptians had stolen from them.

Therefore, the LORD gave Moses HIS divine strategies to recover all that Pharaoh had robbed the children of Israel from, HIS chosen people. HE said unto Moses, HE will give HIS people Israel favour and respect in the sight of the Egyptians that have treated them so cruelly and they will think well of them. So that when they are leaving Egypt, they will give them whatever they ask them for. Every woman should request from her Egyptian neighbour and any other Egyptian woman living in her house, jewels of silver, jewels of gold and clothing. All the items that will be taken from the Egyptians, should be worn on the sons and daughters of the Israelites, when they are leaving Egypt. So that they will take back all the wealth and riches of the Egyptians, plunder them and leave Egypt with great possessions of wealth that are rightfully theirs. Glory be to GOD! Our GOD is a Master Strategist.

What is it that you have lost and you think the situation is hopeless and irredeemable? I am here to let you know that you should not give up hope, neither give up on the GOD of Israel that does not change. HIS word tells us that, HE is the same yesterday, today and forever. What is it that the enemy has robbed you from? Is it your joy, your freedom, your good health, your marriage, your financial prosperity? GOD Almighty, Jehovah El-Elyown the Most High GOD, the Creator of the universe, is able to help you recover back everything the enemy has stolen from you. All you need to do is to make up your mind to say enough is enough to the devil. It is time to take back what the devil stole from me!

The LORD is ready to give us divine strategies to recover all that the enemy has stolen from us and the opportunities we have lost. But we have to seek HIM and put our ears upon HIS chest to listen to HIS divine instructions for total recovery, just like David did.

In 1 Samuel chapter 30 we are told that, David and his men were with king Achish of Gath, in the Philistine's territory when the city of Ziklag was attacked by the Amalekites. By the time they returned back to Ziklag on the third day, the Amalekites had invaded the city, overthrew it and burnt it with fire. They took the women, their children and everyone that was with them captive. The Amalekites did not kill any of their captives but they took them away, with the intention to use them as slaves. Needless to say that David and his men were devastated when they returned to Ziglag and found out what had befallen them. They wept bitterly until they had no more strength to weep. David's two wives at that time Ahinoam and Abigail, were amongst those captured by the Amalekites. You can imagine how distraught David must have been. The people of Ziglag were very sad and disheartened about what had happened to them and their families and blamed David their leader, as the cause of their sorrows. They even discussed stoning him for putting them in that situation. David was described as being "greatly distressed" about the situation. Nevertheless, he did not give up hope but strengthened and encouraged himself in the LORD his GOD.

In the midst of confusion, disappointment and distress, David pulled himself together and sought help from the only wise GOD. He prayed and asked the LORD what to do. He wanted to know whether he should chase after the Amalekites' troop that had invaded their city, destroyed it and held their wives and children captives. The LORD told him to go ahead and pursue them and that he would surely overtake them and, without fail, recover all their enemies has stolen from them. David did what the LORD told him to do and he was able to recover all, exactly as HE had told him. David and his army pursued the Amalekites and defeated them. He recovered his two wives, all they took from them and the spoil of the war, which he shared with his friends, families and the elders of Israel. David recovered all plus the spoil. Hallelujah! I pray that you too shall recover all the enemy has stolen from you, as you look unto the LORD as your helper.

In this new season, we need to fold up our sleeves to fight for what is rightfully ours. Like David, we need to seek the LORD and ask HIM to strengthen and empower us to take back what rightfully belong to us and possess our possessions that are in the hands of the thief. The Lord Jesus told us in John 10:10, that the thief (the devil) comes in order to steal, kill and destroy. But He, Jesus, came that we may have and enjoy life in abundance to the full, till it overflows. You need to make up your mind and remind yourself of where the enemy has stolen from you and be empowered by the Holy Spirit of the living GOD to pursue him to recover all. This is our season and opportunity to walk in a new level of glory and new dimension in the Lord Jesus. He came to give us abundant life. We are expected to live in abundance, walk in abundance and flow in abundance. He is the way, the truth and the life. He will show us the way to divine recovery and divine abundance. I pray that as you make up your mind to seek the LORD with all your heart, may you be strengthened by the power of Holy Spirit of GOD and may He give you divine strategies to recover back your joy, your peace, your family, your children, your opportunities, your businesses, your career, your finances, divine helpers and restore all that the enemy has stolen from you, in the Mighty name of Lord Jesus Christ of Nazareth.

SEVEN
HOW TO STAY FOCUSED IN YOUR NEW SEASON?

1. Repent of Your Sins

To stay focused in this new season, we need to first of all repent of our sins and ask GOD for HIS mercy and forgiveness for all our wrong doings. To repent means to express or feel sincere regret or remorse about one's wrongdoing or sin. According to the online Cambridge dictionary, it also means to be very sorry for something bad you have done in the past and wish that you had not done it.

In Acts 3:19, we are told to repent and turn again, that our sins may be forgiven. The Expanded Bible version explains this verse this way:

"So you must change your heart and life, repent! Come back, return, turn back to GOD, and HE will forgive, wipe out, erase your sins. Then the time of rest, refreshment, comfort, the messianic age will come from the presence of the Lord."

You can see from the above interpretation that we are promised a time of rest, refreshment and comfort, will come from the presence of the Lord, when we repent of our sins.

In 2 Peter chapter 3 we are told that the Lord is not slow to fulfil His promises to us as we count slowness, but He is full of patience towards us, not wishing that any of us should perish but that we should all reach repentance. The Lord Jesus also told us in Matthew chapter 4 that we should repent of our sins for the kingdom of heaven is near. It is time for us to make up our minds and turn away from our old ways and our wrong doings and repent. In this new season, we need to ask for GOD'S mercy, put the past behind us, seek HIS purpose for our lives and renew our minds daily in HIS holy word, so that, we will begin to enjoy the abundant life the Lord Jesus came to give to us and enter into a time of rest, refreshing and comfort in the presence of our GOD.

2. Renew Your Mind

Renewing our minds daily in the word of GOD will also help us to stay focus in this new season. We are in the technological age, which means that we have readily available information at our fingertips. This can be an advantage but could also be a distraction for us if we do not guard and control the type of information we are exposing ourselves to. The word of GOD tells us that we are to guard our hearts with all diligence, from out of it flows the issues of life. This tells me that we are not to allow ourselves to be exposed to all the information that is out there. We need to be careful about where we source our information from and what we watch on television. As Christians, it will be prudent for us to spend time with GOD and HIS word daily, in order for our minds to be renewed. This will also help us to work in GOD'S plan and will for us daily.

The renewed mind is the mind of Christ, it is the transformed mind and it is the repented mind that is ready to embrace the new life in Christ Jesus. It is about seeing things the way the LORD sees them. It is about aligning our thoughts with GOD's thoughts. It's also about having a higher perspectives of life and not having self-defeating thoughts or patterns but embracing the mind of Christ. It is a powerful mind that can change the trajectory of our destiny. 1 Corinthians 2:16b tells us that, we have the mind of Christ. We need to know that we cannot renew our mind by ourselves. We need the supernatural help of the Holy Spirit to renew our minds.

Romans 8:5-6 (NKJV) says:

> "For those who live according to the flesh set their minds on the things of the flesh, but those who live according to the Spirit, the things of the Spirit. For to be carnally minded is death, but to be spiritually minded is life and peace."

3. Seek GOD'S Divine Direction

We need to pray for divine direction so that our steps will always be guided and ordered by the LORD. This will also help us to focus in this new season. When GOD orders our steps we will not be misguided or misled by the enemy. We always need to seek GOD for divine direction so that we will not be deceived and derailed in the journey of life. Even when we fall, are deceived or derailed, we should not stay down but get up, dust ourselves off and continue with the LORD again. For a righteous man falls seven times and still rises up again.

As the world is getting darker, as told in Isaiah Chapter 60 verse 2a, a lot of people are losing their sight both physically and spiritually and are following the wrong path in life. You do not have to look too far to know what I am talking about. Just turn your television set on and you will see the happenings in the world in which we live in now. There are all sorts of atrocities taking place in the world. Atrocities such as the Coronavirus pandemic, famines, pestilences, killings and protestations in the nations of the world, to name a few. But in the midst of these there is hope in Christ Jesus. He is our Deliverer and our Saviour. He will preserve us, protect us and provide for us in the unprecedented time we are in. The continuation of Isaiah 60:2 says that, "but the LORD shall arise upon us and HIS glory shall be seen upon us". See, we have hope in the LORD. It does not matter what is happening in the world right now, the LORD'S word concerning you and me is final. HIS word shall stand and shall come to pass in our lives. That is why we need to ask for HIS divine direction daily in all that we do. For the steps of a good man are ordered by the

LORD. Even in this time of darkness as children of GOD, we should arise and shine in the midst of darkness and shine our light to the world. For we are the light of the world and we have been created by GOD to shine our lights in darkness and to tell the world about the Good News of the Lord Jesus Christ of Nazareth.

4. Pray for Divine Enlightenment

We are to be divinely enlightened about the season and era we are in to maximise our potentials and seize the moment. We need to ask GOD for divine revelation and divine enlightenment in HIS word and through prayer to ascertain our times and seasons. In 1 Chronicles 12:32, we are told that the sons of Issachar had understanding of the times, to know what Israel should do and knew the right time to do it because of their spiritual astuteness all their kinsmen were at their commands.

Now, let us look at what it means to be enlightened. To be enlightened could mean to show understanding, to have sensible ways of dealing with things, to be freed from ignorance and misinformation and (or) it could mean to have full comprehension of the problems involved. According to these definitions of enlightenment, we can see that the sons of Issachar had understanding and full comprehension of the times, of what actions they should take and when to take those actions. Which means they were moving in sync with the plan of GOD for Israel. They were not ahead of GOD nor were they late to execute GOD'S plans for Israel. We too can be enlightened about GOD'S plan and purpose for our nations in which we live in, especially in the times we are in. We need to know how to pray, what to pray for, what to do and when to do what GOD says we should do, for ultimate victory in all that we do. We can also seek HIM for HIS plan and purpose for our lives, families and about the next step to take in our mission for HIM. But this requires us seeking HIM diligently in prayer and waiting on HIM through fasting as HE leads us.

Paul's prayer for the Ephesian believers in Ephesians chapter 1, is that GOD will enlightened the eyes of their understanding, so that they may know what is the hope of HIS calling, and what are the riches of the glory of HIS inheritance in the saints. Why did Paul pray this prayer? It is because, as children of GOD we need to have understanding for GOD'S will for our lives. The eyes of understanding, which I believe is our mind, is to be enlightened about GOD'S will for us, so that we will walk in HIS will for our lives and fulfil HIS purpose. It is important for us believers to know the will of GOD for our lives and do it, to enter into the kingdom of heaven. The Lord Jesus said in Matthew chapter 7, that not every one that says to Him, Lord, Lord, shall enter into the kingdom of heaven but only those that did the will of HIS FATHER which is in heaven.

Ephesians 5:15–20 says:

> "See then that ye walk circumspectly, not as fools, but as wise, redeeming the time, because the days are evil. Wherefore be ye not unwise, but understanding what the will of the Lord is. And be not drunk with wine, wherein is excess; but be filled with the Spirit; speaking to yourselves in psalms and hymns and spiritual songs, singing and making melody in your heart to the Lord. Giving thanks always for all things unto God and the Father in the name of our Lord Jesus Christ."

5. Be Grateful and Thankful unto GOD

Another way we can stay focus in this new season, is by being grateful and being thankful to our GOD daily, for all HIS goodness, loving kindness, faithfulness and tender mercies towards us. HE has been merciful to you and me and has not dealt with us according to the way in which we deserve to be dealt with. We have so many reasons to be thankful. We need to count our blessings and name them one by one and remind ourselves of all the LORD has done for us. If you are alive and you are reading this book, it is enough reason for you to be thankful to our GOD for being counted amongst the living.

We should be thankful to our GOD because everything we have comes from HIM and according to HIS divine power, HE has given unto us all things that pertains unto life and godliness. In Psalm 24, we are reminded that the earth is the LORD'S and all its fullness, the world and all that dwells in it. The heavens are HIS, the earth also is HIS, the world and all that is in it. In addition to this, the Bible also reminds us in John 3:27 that a man can receive nothing except it's given unto him from on high. From these scriptures, you can see some of the reasons why we are to be thankful to our GOD always.

Our GOD is a faithful and righteous FATHER that is incorruptible. Neither can HE be bribed by anyone small, great or mighty. In Revelation 19, we are told that HE is the Faithful and True GOD. HE is a just GOD and HE is no respecter of persons. Only a fool will not serve a GOD like this.

We should be perpetually grateful to HIM for giving us the Lord Jesus, who shed His BLOOD for us at Calvary Cross, died for ALL our sins and gave us ETERNAL life. For Christ also died for our sins once and for all, the just and for the unjust, so that He might bring us to GOD having been put to death in the flesh, but made alive in the spirit (1 Peter 3:18).

Another reason why we should be grateful is because HE is a prayer answering GOD. We should always show our gratitude to him like the leper in Luke 17, that was healed of leprosy by the Lord Jesus. He was not the only leper that the Lord healed, he was one of ten but he chose to come back to glorify the Lord for healing him. Because of his grateful attitude, he was made whole by the Lord. The other nine were healed but were not made whole, except for this grateful leper. This story in the scriptures teaches us to always remember to testify to others about GOD'S goodness in our lives, so that HE will bless us the more.

Most of us thank GOD only when HE has answered our prayers but it should not be so. We should always be thankful to HIM in good times and in difficult times. We should thank HIM not only when HE has given us the victory but also when we need victory from HIM. Especially in hopeless situations, like when the children of Israel were faced with the wall of Jericho. They shouted great shouts of victory unto their GOD and the wall of Jericho fell down flat, and as a result won the battle over Jericho.

God deserves our praise because HE is a present help in time of trouble. Paul and Silas thanked and praised HIM when they were imprisoned by the authorities (the chief magistrates) for delivering the slave girl from the spirit of divination. What happened to them when they gave GOD thanks in advance in the prison? The LORD sent help for them and they were delivered:

> "After striking them many times [with the rods], they threw them into prison, commanding the jailer to guard them securely. He, having received such a

[strict] command, threw them into the inner prison (dungeon) and fastened their feet in the stocks [in an agonizing position]. But about midnight when Paul and Silas were praying and singing hymns of praise to God, and the prisoners were listening to them; suddenly there was a great earthquake, so [powerful] that the very foundations of the prison were shaken and at once all the doors were opened and everyone's chains were unfastened. When the jailer, shaken out of sleep, saw the prison doors open, he drew his sword and was about to kill himself, thinking that the prisoners had escaped. But Paul shouted, saying, "Do not hurt yourself, we are all here!" Then the jailer called for torches and rushed in, and trembling with fear he fell down before Paul and Silas, and after he brought them out [of the inner prison], he said, "Sirs, what must I do to be saved?"

(ACTS 16:23-30)

In the above scriptures we can see the POWER in praising our GOD. When we need deliverance from GOD we need not only pray deliverance prayers, we can be delivered by praising and thanking the LORD Most HIGH. In Psalm 92, we are told that it is a good thing to give thanks unto the LORD and to sing praises unto HIS name. So, in this new season let us decide to be more thankful unto our GOD more than ever before for everything we have, even when things are not going according to our plan. For we know that all things work together for good to them that love GOD and to them who are called according to HIS purpose. We should always remember that GOD ALMIGHTY has BETTER plans for us, because HE knows all things and HE is able to do all things. HE is the ALPHA and the OMEGA and we should give HIM thanks at all times.

The LORD our GOD is the same yesterday, today and forever. HE has not changed. HE is the unchangeable Changer. HE who parted the Red Sea is still doing great and marvellous things in the lives of HIS children. HE will do a new thing in your life today. In Isaiah 43:19 HE said, "Behold, I will do a new thing and now it shall spring forth, shall you not know it? I will even make a way in the wilderness, and rivers in the desert." Ask HIM today to do a new thing in your life, in your marriage, in your relationship, health, children, education, career, finances, ministry, business or whatsoever it may be for you, HE will do it. For HE is FAITHFUL and TRUE (Revelation

19:11b). Also, in a Matthew 7:7-8 He said if we ask we shall receive, if we seek we shall find and if we knock the door will be opened unto us. Why don't you ask HIM to do a new thing in your life and situation today? HE will turn that situation around for you, give you a new opportunity and do the miraculous for you, in the name of Jesus.

Finally, the Bible tells in 1 Thessalonians 5:18 that in "EVERYTHING give thanks: for this is the will of GOD in Christ Jesus concerning you."

EIGHT
PRAYER OF REPENTANCE

I want to give an opportunity to everyone reading this book that has not given their lives to Jesus to do so and make Him their Lord and Saviour today. Romans 10:9 tells us that if we confess with our mouth that Jesus is Lord and believe in our heart that GOD raised HIM from the dead then, we will be saved. Friends, it is that simple. I gave my life to the Lord Jesus over 20 years ago and I can tell you, it was the best thing I have ever done. Knowing Jesus as my Lord and Saviour has kept me alive and sane. The Lord Jesus has given me beauty for ashes.

We are told in Romans 10:13 that everyone who calls upon the name of the Lord will be saved. Today is a good day to give your life to the Lord, for tomorrow might be too late. Remember, we are also told in Romans chapter 6 that the wages of sin is death, but the free gift of GOD is eternal life in Christ Jesus our Lord.

Acts 4:12 says that, there is salvation in no one else, for there is no other name under heaven given among men by which we must be saved but by the name of Jesus. In John chapter 14, the Lord Jesus Himself told us that He is the way, the truth, and the life and that no one comes to the FATHER except through Him. Also, in John 3:3, He tells us that unless one is born again he cannot see the kingdom of GOD. Why don't you give your life to Him today and make Him the Lord of your life? Tomorrow might be too late. You can do it by saying this short, simple and powerful prayer:

> Lord Jesus,
>
> I confess that You are the Lord of my life and I believe in my heart that GOD raised You from the dead. Your word says that anyone who calls upon Your name will be saved. So I confess my sins and repent of them all. Please have mercy upon me and forgive me of all of my sins today. Cleanse me in Your flowing blood that You shed for me on the

cross at Calvary. Write my name in the book of life. Fill me with Your Holy Spirit and let Him begin to direct and guide my steps from this day onwards.

In Your Mighty name Lord Jesus, I pray.

Amen.

Hallelujah! If you have said this prayer and truly believe it, CONGRATULATIONS, you are now saved.

The Scripture tells us in Luke chapter 15 that joy shall be in heaven over one sinner that repents, more than over ninety-nine just persons who need no repentance. You see, the angels are now rejoicing in heaven because you have given your life to the Lord Jesus Christ today. Welcome to the Body of Christ!

Your new season has started in Christ Jesus. As you have, by the grace of GOD, now given your life to Jesus, you must embrace your new life and begin to live for Him. As you have now obtained a new identity in Him, you should start living your life for Him. As you have repented of your sins, you must now turn away from your old ways. This is imperative because there is a huge contrast between your old life and your new life now in Christ Jesus.

Now that you have given your life to Christ, the LORD is expecting you to put off your former conversation of the old man, which is corrupt according to the deceitful lusts and be renewed in the spirit of your mind. You must now cultivate the habit of spending time with the LORD in prayer and by reading HIS word daily to purify yourself and your thoughts as written in Philippians 4:8:

> "Finally, brethren, whatsoever things are true, whatsoever things *are* honest, whatsoever things *are* just, whatsoever things *are* pure, whatsoever things *are* lovely, whatsoever things *are* of good report; if *there be* any virtue, and if *there be* any praise, think on these things."

NINE
DAILY DECREES AND DECLARATIONS FOR TRANSFORMATION IN THE NEW SEASON

Say:

1. I decree and declare in the name of the Lord Jesus Christ, I [put your name here] am a new creation in Christ, old things are passed away behold all things have become new (2 Corinthians 5:17).
2. I decree and declare in the name of the Lord Jesus Christ, there is therefore now no condemnation in me for I [put your name here] am in Christ Jesus, and I walk not after the flesh, but after the Spirit of GOD. For the law of the Spirit of life in Christ Jesus has made me free from the law of sin and death (Romans 8:1–2).

3. I decree and declare in the name of the Lord Jesus Christ, that I [put your name here] cannot be condemned, for Christ Jesus has died for me and HE is risen again. He is even at the right hand of GOD and is also interceding for me (Romans 8:34).
4. I decree and declare in the name of the Lord Jesus Christ, from today I [put your name here] am free forever from unforgiveness, offence and strife. I forgive others as Christ Jesus has forgiven me, for the love of GOD is shed abroad in my heart by the Holy Ghost (Matthew. 6:12; Rom. 5:5).
5. I decree and declare in the name of the Lord Jesus Christ, I [put your name here] have been crucified with Christ. It is no longer I who live, but Christ who lives in me. And the life I now live in the flesh I live by faith in the Son of GOD, who loved me and gave Himself for me (Galatians 2:20).
6. I decree and declare in the name of the Lord Jesus Christ, I [put your name here] am chosen by GOD, to show forth the praises of HIM who has called me out of darkness into HIM marvellous light (1 Peter 2:9).
7. I decree and declare in the name of the Lord

Jesus Christ, that I [put your name here] have been delivered from the law, having died to that which held me captive, so that I serve in the new way of the Spirit and not in the old way of the letter (Romans 7:6).

8. I decree and declare in the name of the Lord Jesus Christ, that my old self was crucified with Christ in order that the body of sin might be brought to nothing, so that I [put your name here] would no longer be enslaved to sin (Romans 6:6).

9. I decree and declare in the name of the Lord Jesus Christ, that I [put your name here] do not conform to this world any longer with its superficial values and customs, but I am being transformed and progressively changed as I mature spiritually by the renewing of my mind focusing on godly values and ethical attitudes, so that I may prove for myself what the will of GOD is, that which is good and acceptable and perfect in HIS plan and purpose for me (Romans 12:2).

10. I decree and declare in the name of the Lord Jesus Christ, I [put your name here] have been saved through faith and not of myself, it is the gift of GOD. Not of works, lest I should

boast, for I am GOD'S workmanship, created in Christ Jesus unto good works, which GOD has before ordained that I should walk in them (Ephesians 2:8 – 10).

11. I decree and declare in the name of the Lord Jesus Christ, that I [put your name here] am not sufficient in myself to think anything as of myself, but my sufficiency is of GOD, Who also has made me able minister of the new covenant, not of the letter but of the Spirit, for the letter kills but the Spirit of GOD gives me life (2 Corinthians 3:5–6).

12. I decree and declare in the name of the Lord Jesus Christ, that in Him all the fullness of Deity (the Godhead) dwells in bodily form completely expressing of the divine essence of GOD. And in Him I [put your name here] have been made complete (achieving spiritual stature through Christ), and He is the head over all rule and authority (of every angelic and earthly power). In Him, I was also circumcised with a circumcision not made with hands, but by the spiritual circumcision of Christ in the stripping off of the body of the flesh (the sinful carnal nature), having been buried with Him in baptism and raised with

Him to a new life through faith in the working of GOD, as displayed when He raised Christ from the dead (Colossians 2:9–12).

13. I decree and declare in the name of the Lord Jesus Christ, that I [put your name here] when I was dead in my sins and in the uncircumcision of my flesh (worldliness, manner of life), GOD made me alive together with Christ, having freely forgiven me of all my sins, having cancelled out the certificate of debt consisting of legal demands which were in force against me and which were hostile to me. And this certificate, the Lord Jesus has set aside and completely removed by nailing it to the cross. When He had disarmed the rulers and authorities (those supernatural forces of evil operating against me), He made a public example of them by exhibiting them as captives in HIS triumphal procession, having triumphed over them through the cross (Colossians 2:13–15).

14. I decree and declare in the name of the Lord Jesus Christ, I [put your name here] have put off the old man with his deeds and have put on the new man, which is renewed in

knowledge after the image of Him that created me (Colossians 3:9–10).

15. I decree and declare in the name of the Lord Jesus Christ, that I [put your name here] have put on the Lord Jesus Christ, and I am making no provision for the flesh to fulfil its lusts (Romans 13:14).

16. I decree and declare in the name of the Lord Jesus Christ, that I [put your name here] with unveiled face, beholding as in a mirror the glory of the Lord, I am being transformed into the same image of the Messiah, from one degree of glory to even more glory, which comes from the Lord, Who is the Spirit (2 Corinthians 3:18).

17. I decree and declare in the name of the Lord Jesus Christ, that I [put your name here] am dead to sin, and my life is hidden with Christ in GOD. When Christ, who is my life, shall appear, then shall I also appear with Him in glory (Colossians 3:3–4).

18. I decree and declare in the name of the Lord Jesus Christ, that I [put your name here] my inner man is being renewed day by day by the Spirit of GOD (2 Corinthians 4:16).

19. I decree and declare in the name of the Lord

Jesus Christ, that I [put your name here] have the mind of Christ to be guided by His thoughts and purposes daily (1 Corinthians 2:16b).

20. I decree and declare in the name of the Lord Jesus Christ, that GOD has not given me [put your name here] the spirit of fear, but of power, and of love, and of a sound mind (2 Timothy 1:7).

21. I decree and declare in the name of Lord Jesus Christ, that in reference to my former nature of life, I [put your name here] lay aside my old self, which is being corrupted in accordance with the lusts of deceit, and I am continually renewed in the spirit of my mind having a fresh, untarnished mental and spiritual attitude, and I have put on the new self, the regenerated and renewed nature, which is created in GOD'S image in the righteousness and holiness of the truth (Ephesians 4:22–24).

Heavenly FATHER,

I thank YOU for my newness in YOU through the Lord Jesus Christ. I thank YOU FATHER for YOUR mercy upon my life. As I start my new life and journey in Christ Jesus this season, let every shame, reproach, sicknesses, diseases, errors, mistakes, delays, limitations, hindrances and frustrations of my former person be rolled and wiped away clean from my life, by the precious Blood of the Lord Jesus now and forever. I receive my newness and YOUR fullness in my life now, by the power of the Holy Spirit, in Christ Jesus that dwells in me.

In the Mighty name of Jesus Christ of Nazareth, I pray.

Amen.

ABOUT THE AUTHOR

Victoria David is the co-founder of Covenant and Glory Ministries International (CGMI) in England, United Kingdom. CGMI is committed to impact the world with the love and grace of GOD. Victoria's passion is to educate others about the transformational power of the word of GOD. She works alongside her husband Pastor Olugbenga David, who is the Senior Pastor of CGMI. Together they are both called with a unique mandate to enlighten their generation about the Covenant of Grace, advance the gospel of Jesus Christ of Nazareth and the Kingdom of GOD.

www.ingramcontent.com/pod-product-compliance
Lightning Source LLC
Chambersburg PA
CBHW050437010526
44118CB00013B/1573